Bitcoin & Black America

Isaiah Jackson

DEDICATION

"Bitcoin is still really new.... look at the reality of what's going on, it makes perfect sense for there to be an unregulated peer-to-peer currency that people can exchange goods and services, without it being linked to a central bank. It's no ulterior motive. It's honest, between the two parties and the transaction is transparent. So, where is the flaw in that?"

Ermias "Nipsey Hussle" Asghedom

Rest in Peace

"The Marathon Continues"

TABLE OF CONTENTS

LAST TO THE PARTY

I was broke as shit. It was October 2013 and working as a high school teacher in the fourth-lowest paying state[1] was taking its toll. I was teaching three periods a day, attending multiple staff meetings, filling out stacks of paperwork, maintaining a computer lab and dealing with teenage emotions on a daily basis. As a public-school teacher I was making around $2600 a month, which was just enough money to be considered broke. To make matters worse, the payment was once a month, so good luck if you had an emergency.

One day, I came home to my roommates who expressed similar concerns with their jobs, finances, and future careers. We all assumed our normal post-work positions on the balcony in our pool-style lounge chairs. There was the familiar sound of beer cans opening and Tame Impala playing in the background when my roommate Brad exclaimed, "I need to make more money." My other roommate and I responded, "Yep I think we all do." We were all entry-level workers in various areas. Brad at an engineering firm, Nick at an investment bank and me, a glorified babysitter. We all threw out ideas.

Real Estate? Not enough to invest.

Stocks? Maybe, but it takes way too much time.

Is there money in Craigslist prostitution?

At this point you can sense our desperation. We kicked around a few more bad ideas and drank a couple more beers. Then my roommate told us his job at an investment bank discussed a new asset class that was forming called Bitcoin. I brushed it off at first, but when he stated that his millionaire parents knew about this technology and planned to invest, I perked up and listened. If I was going to make some money, I needed to follow the moves of someone with money. My roommate said it was too confusing for him, but since I had a technical background, I may be able to understand.

Taking that as a compliment, I took it upon myself to explore this new technology and most importantly, how I could profit from it. When I first looked into Bitcoin I got scared. I looked at the open source code and read the whitepaper in awe and thought, this might work!? So, here's the thing, I'm a natural rebel and I was in college when the financial crisis of 2008 hit the United States economy. I remembered how my peers and I went from broke to broken because of an increase in gas prices, tuition, rent, and books. All due to the mismanagement of credit default swaps in the real estate market from banks. This set off a domino effect which left many people homeless and buried in debt. I was one of those people buried in debt and my curiosity led me to find out how financial institutions can crash an economy because they were too big to fail.

This background knowledge, along with a desperation to get my life together financially, led me to see Bitcoin as a viable option going forward. I followed up my initial research by reading an article on the

"Winklevoss twins". At the time, they were talking about the potential of Bitcoin to rise in value to $100,000 and how they were trying to start an exchange, which would later become the Gemini Digital Assets Exchange.

This piqued my interest and following that, I watched a video of Max Keiser on the "Keiser Report" stating that Bitcoin would change the world and hit a similar price. I was sold at that point! I realized that I could probably make some money using Bitcoin and the icing on the cake was the fearlessness of some person or group called "Satoshi Nakamoto". The whitepaper had a lot of technical components that took me a few reads to understand, but the tone of the paper and the explanation for its creation left me speechless. I definitely should have done more research before I jumped into the Bitcoin market, but I was too broke to care and decided to take a shot. I took $400 out of my struggling savings account and bought my first two bitcoins at the end of October 2013.

Once I had the bitcoins secured on my "wallet.dat" file and had working knowledge about the mechanics of the Blockchain, I let my coins sit on my computer and just stared at my wallet for a week. I was still busy teaching, making lesson plans, writing out learning objectives and studying for a certification. This made research for Bitcoin almost non-existent for a few weeks. Later, I read about Silk Road[2], found a couple of new exchanges and saw the hype for Mt. Gox[3] build on Reddit. Then, in mid-November, I took a look at the Bitcoin charts and saw a price jump from $400 to $750 in one day! Over the next few weeks I saw the price surge to almost $1200 and due to the rush of good news and blogs stating how we would go to the moon, I started picking out my new car and planning vacations to places I couldn't even pronounce. Then it happened.

The price tumbled to around $600 in less than two weeks and slowly fell to the $300 range over the course of a WHOLE YEAR. That's why 2014 was my most important year in cryptocurrency. I learned that the price meant nothing – focus on the technology. Like many people who entered the space in December 2017, I failed to do thorough research on a very complicated subject and threw money at it hoping to get rich. I looked at Bitcoin through the lenses of desperation rather than emancipation. Once I witnessed such a fast-paced rise and fall, I realized that if I wanted to last long in this space, forget the price and focus on how the technology of Bitcoin can make you and people around the world self-sufficient.

In 2014, I did what many people should've been doing in this recent bear market – learning. Over the course of about 18-months I switched jobs, moved to a new city and studied trading, mining and any other subjects pertaining to Bitcoin. Day after day I grew convinced that this technology would change the world and became numb to the constant news and attacks on Bitcoin. By the end of 2014, I learned the basics of cryptocurrency trading and joined a Litecoin mining pool. This helped me learn about the technical aspects of mining software while making residual income outside of my occupation.

March 2015, I finally built up the courage to post something about Bitcoin on social media. My first post was on Instagram and featured a screenshot of Bitcoin's price which was "$247.12". This post along with a few others prompted many people to inquire about Bitcoin and cryptocurrency. I began telling co-workers, family and friends about Bitcoin and how it would financially set them free. I explained how Bitcoin could spark a revolution among regular, working class people. I specifically showed how we could gradually reject fiat currency, use Bitcoin and start our own local economies with a global cryptocurrency.

And nobody cared.

My girlfriend at the time, who was privy to my struggles financially, would inquire "if it's so great why aren't we rich yet?" My uncle, who worked for a bank, shunned my business proposition to purchase Bitcoin ATMs in 2015 because of the "unnecessary risk" involved. Friends I had known for years looked at me differently because they associated Bitcoin with illicit activity due to the Silk Road exchange being shut down. I even had a co-worker state "Well if you are still working here, it must not be that great." It was safe to say, I was once again tested on this new technology and realized:

I don't care.

I didn't care that they couldn't see the potential of Bitcoin, cryptocurrency and blockchain technology. Honestly, it made me realize that I was really on to something because if an idea doesn't scare people then it's not big enough. This pushed me to become a full-time Bitcoin consultant because once people understand Bitcoin, there is no way you can't be excited about the future of currency and global markets. The ability to send money digitally, almost instantly, without the need for a third party is just something you can't ignore.

During this time period of mid-2015, the price of Bitcoin began to gradually rise. I joined the Digital Currency Council, took a Bitcoin course on Udemy and also the Princeton "Bitcoin and Cryptocurrency" course on Piazza. I followed Chris Dunn trading videos and started to follow fellow crypto enthusiasts on Twitter. I started to read more blogs from Bitcoin developers and was even introduced to Ethereum by a friend. The price of Bitcoin didn't matter anymore, and I was doing what I could to educate myself so that I could educate others. Among the black community I started to plan out ways that we could use Bitcoin to our advantage. I found the website "Blacks in Bitcoin" by Edwardo Jackson and started to gain confidence that I wasn't a lone wolf in these crypto streets. I began giving away free satoshis[4] to people while explaining to them how the technology could change their life.

I immersed myself into the cryptocurrency ecosystem.

In mid-2016, I was more knowledgeable, immune to the FUD[5] in the news and officially a HODLer[6]. I sold 0 bitcoins during this time period when the swings in price, coupled with the negative media attention sent many people running for the hills. I can still remember a lot of people who I convinced to buy Bitcoin at $400 selling at $500 because they were unsure about the legality of Bitcoin.

July 2016, I received a call from an old college buddy who noticed my posts on Instagram and decided to ask how I was involved in Bitcoin. We caught up on old times and our conversation was basically:

"So, are you the same Zay?"

"Yep"

"Are you the same King?"

"Hell yea"

"Well, let's do something together with this Bitcoin thing."

The next time we spoke was two weeks later. At the time, I was working as an IT Analyst at a law firm, so I ducked off into an empty office space that was out of view from my boss and discussed how we could have an impact on the Bitcoin community. We realized that the biggest hindrance in the crypto market was access to viable information. Scam coins, fake websites and pyramid schemes were becoming prevalent and we took it upon ourselves to bridge the gap between cryptocurrency and the community. We officially started a cryptocurrency education and consulting firm, KRBE Digital Assets Group.

Working on two different coasts, we consulted dozens of clients from all different backgrounds. Day and night, we both left our jobs and went home to study new developments, exchanges and wallets. Even at work, I was taking a little extra time on my lunch break to watch YouTube videos and stay on top of the market. By early-2017, we saw an explosion of new crypto hedge funds, consulting groups and classes available to retail and institutional investors. The price of Bitcoin crossed $1000 on New Year's Day 2017 and everyone was starting to realize that maybe this new technology wouldn't go away so easily.

Due to a few timely trades, I was able to leave the workforce and I was all-in on cryptocurrency. I did my first "real" presentation about Bitcoin to a crowd of 12

people in January of 2017 and even though the numbers

were small, I knew this is what I wanted to do for the rest

of my life. The mixture of fear, excitement and curiosity

on the faces of that beautiful black crowd made me

realize that what myself and King started would impact a

lot of people if they could just hear about Bitcoin. After

the spike in Bitcoin's price and other emerging

cryptocurrencies like Ethereum and DASH, we finally hit

our stride consulting, trading and investing then

something else happened…

I got hacked.

My email, phone and other sensitive information

were stolen due to the social engineering of family

members and certain precautions not being taken. Just

like the boom and bust cycle of 2013-14, this event made

me realize that being your own bank comes with more responsibility and this market can test your resilience as an investor and even as a human being. I lost business with my side gig of developing websites and access to a couple of wallets that had a small amount of cryptocurrency. I had family members who were receiving fake text messages and being threatened as well. This was a great lesson and at this point I had now survived a bear market, doubt from my peers, and now a hack.

Overall, I was able to manage the hack but as a company, we lost five-figures worth of cryptocurrency due to the inept security of an exchange. It rhymes with Shittrex. Most people would have walked away due to the uncertainty of the market, but people really walk away once they think their life savings can be taken at any time due to an intrusion from an outside source. Money in the bank is insured, but with Bitcoin you have no insurance and take all of the risks. Even though this happened, my belief in a new world shaped by Bitcoin overcame my fear and I went even harder.

King and I realized that working on different coasts caused a rift in our communication and ultimately wouldn't be sustainable. So, I packed up and moved across the country to California two days after the hack happened. Once I arrived, we came up with the idea that we needed to put out video content informing people about crypto news and the market.

We had no name when we started but quickly came up with segments like "Best Altcoins We Buy" and "Bridging the Gap" – a tutorial series about little known crypto subjects. We decided on a name for our current daily show, The Gentlemen of Crypto and we are currently at 400+ shows. Due to the outreach from this show, we are now consulting new clients, broadcast on six different platforms, deliver a podcast via Spotify and iTunes, run a dedicated Lightning Network node, organize local meetups and speak at conferences around the country.

These business ventures along with future endeavors all came as a result of learning about Bitcoin and really studying the technology in order to realize the magnitude of what's taking place. We are literally watching the global financial system change right before our eyes. We have seen people like Jamie Dimon go from calling Bitcoin a "fraud" to creating his own digital currency, JPM Coin. I am glad to say I was alive to see Facebook go from banning all cryptocurrency ads on their platform, to introducing their own digital currency, Libra[7]. Trust me, everything is about to change.

Although my crypto journey will be different from your crypto journey, Bitcoin has a similar effect on most people and that is, it changes your way of thinking. Before Bitcoin, no matter how much money you raised to support a liberation plan, civil rights movement or march, ultimately you have to use the banking system. That barrier is now gone and combined with the ability to communicate globally; cryptocurrency can help the black community like nothing we have ever experienced.

When you finish this book, hopefully you can find a way to implement Bitcoin into your everyday life. Members of the black community should take pride in being innovative and begin building towards a prosperous future using cryptocurrency. Hopefully, during the period of the biggest transfer of wealth in

human history, the black community won't be last to the

party.

CHAPTER 1 | THE BASICS OF BITCOIN

Naval Ravikant once described Bitcoin as "freedom from tyranny and oligarchy dressed up in a get rich scheme." More specifically, Bitcoin is software that allows sending and receiving bitcoins, the world's first cryptocurrency. The invention of Bitcoin is the realization of the "cypherpunk" dream that was started in the early 1990s. Internet privacy for all citizens was the main goal of this group and over the next 15 years, many advancements were made to reach this point. Adam Bach introduced proof-of-work computing[8], Nick Szabo created the term smart contracts[9] and in October 2008,

Satoshi Nakamoto published, "Bitcoin: A Peer-to-Peer Electronic Cash System." This whitepaper introduced a system where any person can send or receive value without the need for a bank or financial institution. Moreover, this document outlined the process for transactions, incentives, proof-of-work and the need for privacy.

After the first coins were mined and sent to Hal Finney[10] in January 2009, the small email list started by Satoshi grew into a network of miners, then users, programmers, and traders. Bitcoin is now a $300+ Billion-dollar industry. Every day new advancements are made to make financial transactions easier through Bitcoin and cryptocurrency.

Popular payment providers like Square, Apple Pay and Samsung Pay all came to the market *after* Bitcoin's invention due to this technological innovation. So, if you use any of those services you can thank the creation of Bitcoin for putting the pressure on companies to provide a simple, secure way of sending money. Most participants in the financial system already use digital currency via bank accounts, phone applications and PayPal. However, those transactions are recorded on a private ledger and bitcoin transactions are recorded on a Blockchain.

What is a Blockchain?

The Blockchain is a digital ledger that is immutable and secure. Much like a database that everyone has access to, the Bitcoin blockchain functions as a decentralized way to verify transactions. Approximately every 10 minutes a "block" of transactions is recorded. To ensure each transaction is valid, the block must link with the block of transactions before with a hash number[11].

The hash number is created with cryptography and represents the data from the previous block. If the block is verified, it is added to the chain of previous blocks i.e. the Blockchain. This process keeps the network secure and makes it very expensive and time-consuming to change the transactions or "hack" the blockchain.

Blockchain technology has become a buzzword for investors and technologists around the globe. Nicknamed "the blockchain stimulus package", the mention of this word sends stocks soaring and makes investors horny just thinking about the potential. The distributed nature of a blockchain makes the transfer of value or information cheaper and more efficient. Companies like Walmart have chosen to test blockchain technology for their supply chain. They have partnered with IBM to improve food safety and cut down on manual processes. Voting, real estate and even social media is starting to implement blockchain technology because of the fundamental use case.

All transactions are recorded by the network and supported by "nodes". According to BitNodes[12], there are 10,499 nodes operating around the world. Anyone who downloads the Bitcoin software and decides to use their computing power is considered a node. There are two basic types of nodes:

Full Node – downloads the entire blockchain and all transactions

Lightweight Client – only records the user's transactions

Some of these full nodes can be configured to become "miners", which is the backbone of the Bitcoin network. If you think about bitcoin miners like gold miners, essentially the more gold miners you have the better chance you have of finding gold. Bitcoin miners use their computing power (tools) to solve complex math problems (ground barrier) and receive bitcoin (digital gold) as the payment. This gives miners incentive to keep the network safe and running 24 hours a day, 7 days a week.

The economic policy of Bitcoin is revolutionary because it has a fixed supply. Only 21 million bitcoins will ever be created and currently over 17 million bitcoins have been mined thus far. The rigid supply coupled with increased demand from consumers will ultimately increase the value of the Bitcoin network. We have a roadmap for production and the last bitcoins will be mined in the year 2140. How did Nakamoto regulate the supply? Well, every 4 years the number of bitcoins paid to miners is halved.

Year	Block Reward (10 minutes)
2009-2012	50 BTC
2012-2016	25 BTC
2016-2020	12.5 BTC
2020-2024	6.25 BTC
2024-2028	3.125 BTC

Known as the "halvening", the next event takes place in May 2020. This design is a creative way to reward early adopters and make the cost of mining and difficulty increase over time.

Why is Bitcoin Important?

Fiat currency is printed by The Federal Reserve at-will. Next, they circulate the money to banks and private institutions that decide who can receive loans for housing, school and business. This process is inefficient and has allowed private groups to control the U.S. money supply for over 100 years. Over time, the Federal Reserve has tried to maintain a 2% core inflation rate because we expect to see rising prices over time. However, we all know this process has not been beneficial to black Americans and has made our middle class nearly non-existent due to stagnant wages and higher prices[13].

Inflation affects people over many generations, so it's hard to notice. Now that you know, it should be clear that we are pawns in a bigger financial game. It's like the old tale about the frog in the pot. If you turn the heat up too fast on a frog in water, it will boil, the frog will sense danger and jump out. However, if you slowly turn the heat up over a long period of time, by the time the frog notices, he is already cooked. We have been slowly "cooked" with inflation. Take into account the historically racist policies dedicated to keeping black people economically shut out and you can start to see why Bitcoin is important for black people.

What Gives Bitcoin Value?

Andreas Antonopolous branded Bitcoin "The Internet of Money", which accurately describes this form of new currency. Bitcoin is valuable as a currency because it is a store of value, unit of account and medium of exchange.

The ability to use a Bitcoin as a long-term investment without the interference of a third-party also has a high-value proposition. Since Bitcoin hit exchanges in 2010, speculators and investors have driven the price of Bitcoin from $0.06 to $9,733 during the writing of this book. Simply put, Bitcoin is the best performing asset in the world over the past decade.

Inventing a new form of currency does not come without hardships. Over the past nine years, Bitcoin has been labeled as currency only used for "illicit activities," banned by governments, scolded by bankers and misrepresented by scammers. Bitcoin represents a new form of competition for the financial industry and supporters of the legacy system have worked to discourage adoption of cryptocurrency worldwide. Even so, respected industry titans like Steve Wozniak, Elon Musk and Richard Branson have praised Bitcoin's revolutionary technology. The demand for Bitcoin comes from many different sectors and the black community needs to engage in this financial revolution.

If any group of people should recognize how media can misrepresent you because they feel threatened, it should be the black community. Bitcoin and the black community are a match made in heaven. Even people *outside* of our community recognize the ability of the black community to free themselves with Bitcoin. Max Keiser, host of the Keiser Report, and notable white man stated "I told America's black community to load up on Bitcoin in 2011. If they had, they'd be able to buy the white community by now." While I don't share his sentiment about buying the white community, we absolutely can rebuild our own community while working to create brand new communities worldwide.

Before 2009, you could protest, raise money, and start a business but since you had to deposit your money into banks, you continued to feed a system that does not have our best interests at heart. All of those deposits would enrich banks who encouraged redlining, denied loans to qualified applicants and even beyond race, bankrupted the entire financial system in 2008. Then, they gave themselves bonuses to celebrate! We will discuss the specifics in a later chapter, but ultimately, you can't build a strong community without your own currency.

Cryptocurrencies and Tokens

The invention of Bitcoin opened Pandora's box of financial freedom in the form of cryptocurrencies. Since Bitcoin's inception, there have been thousands of cryptocurrencies and tokens created. These inventions have allowed programmers, financial institutions and cryptographers to collaborate on projects that will forever change our vision of global economic policy. It is important to remember that cryptocurrencies and tokens are different. Let's explore why they are both important to the future of the monetary system.

Cryptocurrencies are digital coins that have similar properties to Bitcoin. They each have their own blockchain, open source technology, a rigid supply and the ability to send and receive value. When cryptocurrencies are first created, they can be mined or purchased with Bitcoin. Each coin has a trading pair available on an exchange and most coins have historically gained thousands of percent in value.

Mining is one big difference between Bitcoin and other cryptocurrencies. Like we discussed earlier, Bitcoin uses proof-of-work to verify transactions on the blockchain. Other coins like Ethereum, started out using proof-of-work but will be migrating to proof-of-stake. The goal of both algorithms is the same, but instead of mining power determining who receives the block reward, proof-of-stake rewards users based on their stake in the coin. The more you own, the more you earn. This gives consumers the incentive to buy ether and hold long-term.

When Ethereum was first created, the founder, Vitalik Buterin established a decentralized autonomous organization (DAO) that raised over $150 million. This is another fundamental difference between other cryptocurrencies and Bitcoin. Founders who are not anonymous and raising capital are both properties of new cryptocurrencies. Many projects followed the path of Ethereum and developed a way to raise money on their platform using smart contracts and initial coin offerings (ICOs). The frenzy that happened as a result of this new invention led to thousands of ICOs in the following years, with 2017 and 2018 being the best years for raising funds. The average ICO raised about $24 million each and the total investment surpassed $11 Billion[14].

Litecoin is perhaps the most popular cryptocurrency for payments besides Bitcoin. Since its inception in 2011, Litecoin has grown to a $7 Billion market cap. Charlie Lee created this coin with the intention of giving users a reliable second option for cryptocurrency payments. He tweaked the design to have 2.5-minute block times compared to 10 minutes for Bitcoin. Fees are usually cheaper as well, so many people prefer to use Litecoin when sending and receiving value. Some people have described Litecoin as just the test net for Bitcoin, but it has proven its value with a strong community supporting the project.

Privacy coins are a valuable asset to the cryptocurrency ecosystem. They allow consumers around the world to transact privately and securely. The need for immutable, private transactions will become more necessary as governments around the world try to ban cryptocurrencies. Countries such as Venezuela and India have both issued an outright ban of cryptocurrencies and punish citizens for using them. When you use a coin like

Monero, they use ring signature technology[15] to ensure that each transaction has plausible deniability. The account keys needed to send value use a "ring" of possible signers and outside observers cannot trace it back to one private key. This innovation gives hope for a future where anyone can transact privately without the need for unnecessary "know-your-customer "(KYC) standards. Other coins such as Zcash and Cryptic Coin have the same goal. They allow users to transact privately but have a slight difference in each project. No matter your coin of choice, black Americans need to make sure we keep these options available.

Digital tokens are different from cryptocurrencies because they do not usually have their own blockchain. Instead, they are built on an available platform like Ethereum and are a digital representation of value. How are tokens distributed? The ICO craze that I mentioned earlier has been the way that most projects raise money and issue digital tokens to investors. More specifically, when investors want to support a project, they can use ether to purchase tokens at a set price. When the investment period is over, investors are issued their digital tokens which can be used for trading or utility for the project.

The most common type of token on the market is the ERC-20 token issued on the Ethereum platform. The name may seem scary, but it is simply a standard proposed by Buterin to make token creation relatively easy. Any coin with this distinction has the same 6 functions. Every ERC-20 token must have a total supply, a token balance, ability to transfer, transfer to one another, approvals and an allowance of tokens to withdraw.

Some of the most popular tokens on the market are Maker ($MKR), Binance Coin ($BNB) and 0x ($ZRX). Each token has its own function however they adhere to the same standard to ensure security and consumer confidence. Lamar Wilson and Lafe Taylor are black developers who created an ERC-20 token called "CJs", after the great Madame C.J. Walker. Smaller denominations are referred to as "Garvey's" after Marcus Garvey to remind users of our rich history. This token has gotten support from thousands of black investors who want to use a native currency for payments. There is even a decentralized marketplace where you can build a store, freelance or crowdfund with this token[16].

Bitcoin Wallet

A bitcoin wallet displays your bitcoins value, keeps a record of the blockchain and allows sending and receiving value. Your wallet always contains two keys, public and private. Your public key is a string of numbers, much like a phone number, that can be changed at-will and broadcast to others to receive payment. The public key is derived from the private key and thanks to the power of cryptography, can be generated multiple times for every wallet.

The private key is like your Social Security number. Never give this information away because your funds can be stolen. If you have a lockbox at a bank, you need your personal key and the banker has a key to open your lockbox. The public and private key function the same way with being able to send and receive funds.

There are four main types of wallets available for consumers including desktop wallets, phone wallets, hardware wallets and paper wallets. Each type of wallet has its pros and cons however each person can have as many wallets as they want. I would recommend having at least one of each to diversify your holdings and prevent you from a single point of attack. Here are a few wallet choices available:

Desktop Wallet	Phone Wallets	Hardware Wallets	Paper Wallets
Green Address	BitMari	Ledger Nano	https://bitcoinpaperwallet.com/
Electrum	BRD Wallet	Trezor	https://www.bitaddress.org/
Exodus	Blockchain	OpenDime	

Exchanges (Fiat-to-Crypto)

Exchanges are platforms that allow trading of cryptocurrency between two parties. The exchange itself is usually the seller/buyer that you interact with for the transaction. However, there are some exchanges that allow peer-to-peer trading using methods like cash, Zelle and Amazon Gift Cards to purchase cryptocurrency. Different exchanges have different fee structures, custodial services and varying digital assets available for purchase. Here are a few of the top exchanges:

U.S. Exchanges	International Exchanges
Coinbase	BitPesa | Kenya
Uphold	Coin Direct | South Africa
Gemini	NairaEx | Nigeria
Local Bitcoins	Binance | Malta
Paxful	Huobi | Singapore

Exchanges (Crypto-to-Crypto)

Bitcoin exchanges allow buying and selling with fiat currency. However, many of the other cryptocurrencies available in the market can be purchased with Bitcoin ($BTC), Ethereum ($ETH), stablecoins and exchange coins like Binance ($BNB). These new currency pairs can be accessed using a variety of websites that allow trading and the ability to deposit/withdraw funds to that coin's native wallet. These exchanges usually have 100s of trading pairs available and offer promotional items, news and phone app access. Here are a few examples of crypto-to-crypto exchanges that are well known in the industry.

Binance www.binance.com
Bittrex www.bittrex.com
Poloniex www.poloniex.com
Kucoin www.kucoin.com
IDEX www.idex.market

Bitcoin ATMs

Over-the-counter (OTC) trading of Bitcoin and cryptocurrency is still risky for some consumers, but Bitcoin ATMs can facilitate a transaction of buying or selling cryptocurrency. These kiosks offer a solution to the unbanked or cash-rich citizens who want privacy when using cryptocurrency. According to Coin ATM Radar, there are currently 5016 ATM machines operating worldwide. Many ATM providers have added the functionality to purchase other cryptocurrencies including but not limited to, Ethereum, Litecoin, Bitcoin Cash and ZCash.

The addition of new coins along with an increasing market adoption rate makes this a viable option to do business when dealing with cryptocurrencies. Here are a few Bitcoin ATM providers[17]:

| Genesis Coin www.bitcoinatm.com |
| Lamassu www.lamassu.is |
| Bit Access www.bitaccessbtm.com |
| General Bytes www.generalbbytes.com |

Regulations

The invention of Bitcoin opened up Pandora's box of innovation and produced cryptocurrency, tokens, digital currency and stablecoins. All of these blockchain-based forms of money have been hard to define and that has produced a wide variety of regulations from U.S. agencies. These agencies include the Securities and Exchange Commission (SEC), Financial Crimes Enforcement Network (FinCEN) and the Commodity Futures Trading Commission (CFTC). Since Bitcoin is considered "virtual currency" by the agencies listed above, they have taken it upon themselves to provide regulatory standards for everyone involved in this industry.

These agencies have implemented various laws

and practices to regulate the cryptocurrency industry.

Now that various government agencies consider Bitcoin

"real" money, you know the Internal Revenue Service

has to get their slice of the pie. They have taken a

reasonable approach with cryptocurrency taxes and

provide a legal framework similar to what we have now

with stocks and bonds. Make sure to connect with an

experienced tax professional and accountant to determine

your tax liability for the year. Rebecca Samuels is a black

Certified Public Accountant (CPA) in the Washington

D.C. area. Her company, Pythagus LLC, specializes in

crypto taxes and is just one of many resources for people

to use during tax season.

Candidates for political office are using Bitcoin

donations to help their campaigns as well. We will go

into more detail in a later chapter but from a regulation

standpoint, the Federal Election Commission has put out clear guidelines to politicians about contributions in cryptocurrency.

Other agencies such as the Consumer Financial Protection Bureau (CFPB) and the U.S. Government Accountability Office have taken steps to make sure illegal activities such as gambling and Ponzi schemes are not allowed in the Bitcoin industry[18]. They have also published tips on how to spot a scam or dishonest company so that consumers can make informed decisions about "virtual currency."

Everyone in the black community who plans to enter this industry should take a look at these various documents. You don't have to become an expert, but you can protect yourself and family by having a grasp on the basic regulations put forth by the government. Here are the current rules they have implemented:

Securities and Exchange Commission (SEC)	- Bitcoin is not considered a security - Initial Coin Offerings (ICOs) may be considered security offerings and fall under the SEC's jurisdiction
Financial Crimes Enforcement Network (FinCEN)	- Exchange administrators are subject to the Bank Secrecy Act and must register as a Money Services Business
Commodity Futures Trading Commission (CFTC)	- Declared Bitcoin a "commodity" in 2014 and enforces the law with unregistered futures exchanges
Internal Revenue Service (IRS)	- Treats virtual currency like property and imposes capital gain tax
Federal Election Commission (FEC)	- Up to $100 in Bitcoin Donations - Know Your Customer (KYC) information like name, address and occupation must be provided

Join the Bitcoin Network

This is not a technical book, but much like driving a car, you don't need to know how to change your transmission or fix a head gasket in order to drive. Small tasks like putting in gas and using your turn signals are comparable to the simple task of downloading a wallet, buying from an exchange and using Bitcoin for payments. Even if you don't want the hassle of buying or selling cryptocurrency you can show your support by downloading a full node and wallet. This keeps the network decentralized and ultimately makes the Bitcoin network more secure.

Joining the Bitcoin community is a simple process, however, staying in the community requires a change in your way of thinking. Investment in traditional markets has been traditionally low among the black community and many people missed an opportunity to invest in startups such as Google, Facebook and Apple. This was due to a lack of education, lack of finances or both. Never again. These two subjects should be at the forefront of our mindset going into the future. We have to put a premium on learning about finances and technology to ensure our economic survival in America. Doing your part to join the Bitcoin network is a great first step and the black community has to start today.

Now that you have learned this information, congratulations! You are now in the "1%" of world citizens who have basic knowledge about Bitcoin and cryptocurrency. Once you get involved by running a full node or using an exchange you will be able to say you joined a revolution. We can use this change in the financial world to enrich ourselves and provide generational wealth and knowledge. Let's start by building a 21st century economy.

CHAPTER 2 | 21ST CENTURY ECONOMY

The black community has a rich history of entrepreneurship. During the years between 1900-1930, we entered what historian Juliet Walker called the "golden age of black business" because the number of businesses in the black community doubled[19]. Forced segregation made black customers spend their money at black-owned businesses. The combination of racism from banks, white business owners and police forced us to circulate the black dollar amongst ourselves.

We have started a new golden era of black business with over 400% growth in black businesses in 2018[20]. Our ancestors had no way to predict that one day we could have sovereign money that doesn't require permission, but I can almost guarantee they would use Bitcoin if given the chance 80 years ago.

The circulation of the black dollar is almost non-existent compared to other communities. The Asian dollar is estimated to circulate 120 times more than the black dollar which stays in our community an average of 6 hours[21]. As a resident of Los Angeles, I frequently visit Koreatown, Little Ethiopia etc. and they are thriving. They prosper even though most of the business's names are in their native language! If we shifted our entrepreneurial mindset to accepting Bitcoin, we would essentially make outside communities adjust to our preferred payment method. We should let Bitcoin and cryptocurrency be our economic "language" and force other businesses to get down or lay down as Beanie Siegel so eloquently explained.

Peer-to-peer (P2P) payment systems, such as Bitcoin, make each person inherently entrepreneurial. Buyers and sellers can transact with or without a third party and using Bitcoin, you don't need permission to start. Unbanked citizens, entrepreneurial kids and others who are shut out from the banking system can start their own business and wallet. Since 2010, the development of wallets, security and exchanges have made it easier than ever to accept Bitcoin.

Entrepreneurial fervor mixed with the freedom of Bitcoin has created a perfect storm of innovation for the black community. The participation of everyone is the goal, but we have to play our part. The 21st century economy that I envision has four main groups:

Consumers | private citizens that make purchases

Sellers | private citizens who occasionally sell goods

Jobs and Careers | employees to a company

Business Owners | entrepreneurs who run a business

Consumers

Circulation of the "black dollar" between businesses and consumers has been the goal of black entrepreneurs for years. The new digital economy has produced a new way to buy goods with Bitcoin and cryptocurrency. I propose that we kill two birds with one stone and use some, if not most, of our "black dollars" to withdraw from the hyperinflated banking system, acquire Bitcoin and circulate that wealth amongst our black businesses.

This change in doing business begins with consumers. Some may think that if they see businesses accept Bitcoin then people will acquire Bitcoin to make payments. However, I believe that business owners are less likely to take on the risk of accepting a historically volatile currency without demand from consumers. In fact, volatility decreases once consumers are willing to make payments for everyday products, lowering risk for business owners[22].

Black households have the lowest median wealth amongst races in America[23]. If we don't have much money, the best way to acquire what you need is to increase your spending power or more plainly, buying more for less. In our current economy, the value of the dollar decreases every year due to inflation making your buying power increasingly less. Remember 10 cent burgers? Less than $1 gas? Those days are never coming back due to the built-in inflation that makes you have to constantly work to make more money but end up with generally the same amount of goods. What would happen if the money you spent increased in value over time due to the consensus of the other people who wanted to spend that currency as well? This is how good money works.

The utility value of Bitcoin and the consensus among the black community to use digital currency can be a self-fulfilling prophecy. Let me explain, if we acquire Bitcoin as consumers and *prefer* to use Bitcoin instead of the dollar, mainstream adoption of Bitcoin payments will occur among black-owned businesses, which raises demand and the value of Bitcoin. Outside communities who want to do business with the black community will have to adjust to our preferred crypto economy, which raises demand, increases the value of Bitcoin, and ends with the consumer's buying power increasing.

In a deflationary economy a consumer can spend bitcoins but retain their US dollar value because of the increase in value. This works best when consumers use Bitcoin during a bull market[24], so we will focus on a 7-month period from January 2017 to July 2017. We can test this theory with two simple parameters:

- 1 BTC purchased on January 1st = $996.34

- Spend 0.1 BTC each month

January	Spend 0.1 BTC = $99.63
February	Spend 0.1 BTC = $98.52
March	Spend 0.1 BTC = $122.81
April	Spend 0.1 BTC = $109.35
May	Spend 0.1 BTC = $144.35
June	Spend 0.1 BTC = $241.54
July	Spend 0.1 BTC = $245.70
TOTAL	Spent 0.7 BTC or $1,061.90

This chart shows a constant rate of purchases at the monthly average Bitcoin price. We can conclude that over this 7-month period, using Bitcoin as a payment system allowed you to purchase *more* than you originally spent for the 1 BTC, while still retaining a balance of 0.3

BTC (Valued at $3700 | June 26, 2019).

This example shows an increase in spending power, a savings balance for the future and a show of support for black-owned businesses who decided to accept Bitcoin as payment. A self-fulfilling prophecy indeed.

It's important to remember that this is a new technology, so Bitcoin is not a completely reliable medium of exchange. However, if Bitcoin will become a global payment system, black consumers must start the process of purchasing goods with cryptocurrency now. Projects like Guapcoin[25] started by "Tavonia Evans" addresses the issue of circulating cryptocurrency among the black community. Bitcoin is the most popular cryptocurrency for storing value, but this project aims to circulate the "black dollar" and support black-owned businesses. There is a dedicated $GUAP wallet and

Masternodes available for purchase. These Masternodes provide the backbone of the project by paying owners in $GUAP as an incentive for validating payments. If you shop at black-owned businesses, solutions like Guapcoin allow consumers to disconnect from the traditional banking system and start to build a strong community with cryptocurrency as the foundation. Business owners can sign-up to use $GUAP today, but consumers should lead the charge and ask businesses to accept this coin alongside Bitcoin.

Individual Sellers

When you decide to sell goods as a private citizen, you can barter, accept cash or digital payments. These new technological advancements have made the transfer of value easier than ever. Bitcoin and cryptocurrency are quickly becoming the new ways to transfer value between two parties. Bitcoin's current use case is predominantly speculative and a store of value but accepting cryptocurrency as a medium of exchange is the easiest way to accumulate and use for later purchases.

Selling goods via Craigslist, Offer Up or at a local yard sale are great use cases for accepting Bitcoin. The black community needs all the options available to generate wealth. Even as an individual seller, we should open up our customer base and accept cryptocurrency. As the economy becomes more decentralized, sellers should look to using decentralized platforms as well. The opportunity to learn about the site, gain customers and help build the new economy is priceless.

Software programs like Open Bazaar[26] allow sellers to build a store and accept cryptocurrency for payment. Other platforms like Bit Happy[27] allow

individual sellers to freely do business with others by

connecting your internet browser. Don't underestimate

the power of marketing to the Bitcoin community. Often

times, many loyal users prefer using bitcoin over fiat

currency because it helps move the community forward.

If members of the black community can begin to engage

in this practice, we can attract that customer base.

Service workers who accept tips for bartending,

car washes, Uber etc. should take the time to print a QR

code from a trusted wallet and give customers the option

to tip you in Bitcoin. Most consumers do not use Bitcoin

on a regular basis, but if they hear "I accept Bitcoin"

from every black person when they have to give a tip,

they will explore for themselves. For the consumers who

do hold Bitcoin this is an opportunity to grow your

network and possibly receive bitcoin for a tip.

The question of how you should distribute your bitcoin and fiat holdings can be left up to you. However, the black community should store a portion of our profits in our choice of cryptocurrency. We have only seen the beginning of how valuable this crypto economy can become.

Sellers should position themselves to reap the rewards of a good money system gaining value over time. Bitcoin payment providers such as GoCoin allow the seller to determine what percentage of the sale can remain in Bitcoin or fiat. For example, if you sell a $100 product, you can elect to keep 20% in Bitcoin and cash the rest out minus fees. Other payment providers like Coin Payments allow 100s of cryptocurrency options with automatic conversion to the coin of your choice. If you actually believe that you should have an immutable, secure way to transfer value then I propose we start this process now.

Jobs and Careers

This generation has the highest number of black college graduates in American history[28]. This has allowed us to have black representation in a number of jobs. Although our median wealth has stayed the same since the 1960s, we have seen various careers get more populated by black workers[29]. As our economy begins to change and implement cryptocurrency, I propose that members of our community do two things to set ourselves up for future generations:

1.   Accept payment for work in Bitcoin and cryptocurrency

2.   Implement Bitcoin and blockchain technology into your career field

Accept Payment in Bitcoin

Companies such as Bitwage[30] allow employees to get paid in Bitcoin. They allow you to transfer your paycheck using a seamless process and quick registration plan. It would be irresponsible to ask black people to accept only Bitcoin at this time. Nevertheless, learning this process now and testing it out a few times will enable us to use this technology in the future. If there is a time period where Bitcoin can become pegged to a nation's currency and payments are adopted in the mainstream, we can have the tools necessary to accept a salary in Bitcoin if necessary.

In numerous black neighborhoods, check cashing businesses have taken wealth out of our community. By charging a fee to deposit a paper check or just to get your own damn money, they make money off your hard work.

By comparison, getting paid in Bitcoin and cryptocurrency only requires a small network fee. The volatility of Bitcoin's price is well documented but accepting payment can actually increase your USD holdings, cancelling out the small fee from a third party such as Bitwage. The value of your dollar is not capable of increasing in value at the rate of Bitcoin, but it does provide a stable unit of account. This means that we should be savvy in our use of Bitcoin and the dollar while we build an economy where we can be mostly crypto-based. We have to start playing the long game and make sure we own a piece of the Bitcoin pie.

Don't hesitate to ask your employer if you can be paid in Bitcoin or cryptocurrency! I realize most employers will give you a confused look and probably not agree, but it starts the conversation. Furthermore, if co-workers start to request payment in Bitcoin then you may see them reconsider their stance. With the addition of Bitcoin to payroll and tax software it is becoming easier to compensate employees with Bitcoin or the cryptocurrency of their choice.

Implement Bitcoin and Blockchain technology

Every black-owned company doesn't need a blockchain but almost all careers can implement Bitcoin payments. Knowledge of both subjects for black professionals will give us a community-wide boost in the new digital economy. Currently, the market share for most careers that have blockchain-related clients is very small and we need to get in at the ground floor. Numerous jobs and careers are starting to see the demand for companies who specialize in this industry. We have to position ourselves to do the same no matter your chosen field. Some of the best examples where we can implement Blockchain technology include accountants, lawyers and engineers.

The demand for accountants who can handle blockchain-based companies is growing every day. Blockchain-based companies who have to balance their books and pay taxes are looking to give their business to anyone who knows about the industry and can provide solutions. Black CPAs and other traditional accountants can learn about cryptocurrency through various platforms such as the Digital Currency Council. If black accountants can provide this service to a growing community, we can also have an influence on regulations put forth by the SEC, IRS, FINRA and others. Once cryptocurrency becomes mainstream and accountants are *required* to have this knowledge, our community will be one step ahead and not only have the knowledge, but the experience to demand more money for our service.

Lawyers who specialize in blockchain-related business are needed in order to grow a strong Bitcoin community. Since this industry reaches into corporate, real estate, and marriage, I encourage black lawyers to start building that foundation now. If you work for a law firm or run your own firm, helping implement this into the business plan can produce an influx of business. You will have the knowledge available to service them, which can lead to more work and ultimately more wealth flowing into our community.

Divorce and child support lawyers definitely need to be well-versed in cryptocurrency[31]. In the near future we will see thousands of new cases that will involve people using a different type of money to transact business. For example, in the current law, child support is taken from the mother or father's paycheck and distributed to the other party. What happens when the payer starts to accept a private cryptocurrency and claims to make less than before? Where will you get proof? How do you contact exchanges or use a block explorer to find the movement of money? These are all issues that will move black lawyers to the front of the pack if we can start to represent our people on these matters.

When couples divorce and need to split their estate, lawyers who can identify cryptocurrency holdings for their client and claim them in a court of law will increase their status in this field. Not only will your client need you to understand how this industry works, but a lack of knowledge on Bitcoin and cryptocurrency can also make you less desirable as a divorce lawyer in the future. These are a few examples, but I encourage all black lawyers to educate yourself on Bitcoin and blockchain technology as it pertains to your field.

Learning the basic languages of building software is important, but black engineers should begin to focus on building blockchain products and crypto-friendly software. This industry has a high demand and most companies are paying 27% more than the market salary of traditional software engineers[32]. The new applications and financial systems will be built on the blockchain. Let's focus our energy on being at the forefront of this revolution, enrich ourselves and build the technology that other consumers will use.

The current tech space has thousands of apps available on iPhone and Android, but decentralized apps are starting to become popular. Also known as "Dapps", new games, smart contracts and collectible platforms are shaping the future of phones and tablets. Most Dapps are not ready for production but platforms such as NEO, Ethereum and Ubiq allow development from anyone. Black developers are finally starting to receive roles at top companies such as Apple and Google, but we can start to pivot our energy towards building the applications or Dapps of the future. This will bring the market to us and give us leverage in the 21st century economy as the new "builders."

Business Owners

The amount of new black-owned businesses that operate mostly online is staggering. Industries such as clothing, jewelry, marketing, and books are available online and convenient for shoppers worldwide. At the very least, adding another form of payment like Bitcoin will open your market up to international exposure.

Bitcoin users around the globe use directories to make payments with Bitcoin instead of fiat currency. Websites like Spend Bitcoins and Bitcoin Radar list companies that specifically accept Bitcoin. Other websites like BitRefill allow you to purchase gift cards at top companies with Bitcoin. Black business owners can list their company on that platform and gain exposure there as well.

For businesses who have a website, WordPress provides various plug-ins that allow you to accept Bitcoin payments. They also accept Bitcoin as payment to use their platform. If you create a website that sells goods or services, talk to your developer and see how to implement an option for Bitcoin payments. Companies like BTC Pay Server provide solutions for online businesses to accept Bitcoin. If you truly believe in building a 21st century economy, you have to use all the tools available and accepting Bitcoin for payments is a step in the right direction.

Traditionally, most stores with a brick and mortar location have a bulky, expensive point-of-sale system.

These systems are slowly phasing out and lighter, cheaper machines like the Square POS are starting to be used. Square payments have a Bitcoin option available at some locations and will probably be implemented everywhere in the next few years.

I propose that alongside this system you implement a low-cost solution for processing Bitcoin payments in-person. Companies such as Coingate and Pundi X allow business owners to process cryptocurrency payments with a dedicated point-of-sale system. As soon as you advertise that you accept Bitcoin usually two things happen. First, customers will ask "what is Bitcoin?" which sparks the conversation necessary to get people educated on the subject. Most black consumers haven't even heard the word "Bitcoin" or "cryptocurrency" and when a trusted business mentions these words consumers will research for themselves.

Second, local Bitcoin enthusiasts who would rather pay with Bitcoin will start to visit your store, increasing traffic and most likely profit. Many people who are members of the Bitcoin community understand that circulation of this currency will only help with adoption.

Businesses like barbershops and hair salons are prevalent in the black community so let's start there and describe how they can benefit. Let's say you own one of these businesses, every day you have to take in a lot of cash and then deposit it manually into a bank account. Some of these stores have even begun using point-of-sale options like Square to process digital transactions. These shops can advertise that they accept Bitcoin and cryptocurrency. Having a point-of-sale system to facilitate these payments allows black business owners to take advantage of free exposure, no chargebacks and a decrease in risk associated with most cash businesses.

Furthermore, tips between the barber or hair stylist and the customer are essentially peer-to-peer payments. Having a QR code available to accept Bitcoin can reduce the amount of cash on hand and give patrons another option for payment. I am not suggesting we throw out all traditional methods of accepting payment, but in order to prepare ourselves and future generations for the 21st century economy these steps should be taken in our community.

Facebook and other platforms such as Shopify have created an e-commerce economy that allows people to start a side business without much resistance. Uber Eats, Postmates, Easy Shift and other software platforms have created an economy where people can become a part-time entrepreneur using just a cell phone. Since we have this economy currently, the natural next step is to implement a payment system that benefits us long-term. Becoming innovators in the Bitcoin and blockchain payment space is imperative. If we want to become competitive, or dare I say, dominant in the future global market, black people around the globe need to prepare for the next 100 years.

If we can establish a strong foundation testing and using Bitcoin in our community, we will have the ability to dictate the rules and regulations of the future digital economy. Many government officials and lawmakers do not have the experience with Bitcoin to understand how it is used. As more information is presented before Congress and committees, their knowledge will grow but they will need the help of community leaders, business owners and Bitcoin users. Our knowledge will put us in a position to give advice on how to implement a fair and secure use of blockchain technology. We no longer need to fight for a seat at the financial table, we can build the table with Bitcoin, cryptocurrency and a 21st century economy.

CHAPTER 3 | EDUCATION

Bitcoin combines the hardest parts of finance and technology so it will be challenging to educate yourself. However, learning the basics of Bitcoin and cryptocurrency will enable you to share tidbits of information with the children in your life. When they have pressing questions about "money" or how to make purchases you can explain all of the options available. Children are our future and if we want to build a prosperous community, we have to begin the Bitcoin education early. Kids are sponges who soak up all the information around them so as a parent, uncle, aunt or guardian it is our responsibility to teach them.

Often times children are taught the basics of money with small amounts of change. They can comprehend basic addition and subtraction and as they grow older use the concepts of fractions and decimals. The traditional ways of teaching math in school may continue, but if you want to use an alternative method, why not let them see a ledger of Bitcoin transactions to see how this works in action. All cryptocurrency ledgers contain inputs and outputs of funds in each wallet. Showing children how this works will create a foundation of Bitcoin knowledge as they grow and learn more. Once kids reach middle school age, explaining how the price of Bitcoin is compared to the US dollar will supplement their knowledge about decimals and fractions. Market cap and percent gains can also be applied when teaching school-age children the basics of a market.

From a technological standpoint, I would suggest putting children in programs that teach them how to code. Even though children can process the basic aspects of Bitcoin from a mathematical standpoint, we have to help kids learn about technology, so they can help build the future we want to see created. Once kids can pick up basic coding concepts and learn how to use everyday technology, we can supplement that knowledge with Bitcoin basics.

Building applications and mining are two things that school-age children can be exposed to at an early age. Using a Raspberry Pi with basic commands to show how mining cryptocurrency works is one example. They can apply their knowledge about the crypto market, grow up in an environment where Bitcoin is applied to real life and build the next applications needed for mainstream adoption.

Millions of black children attend summer camps after school has finished for the year. Summer programs that cater to a majority black population need to implement a Bitcoin and blockchain course or curriculum. The concepts of Bitcoin that are discussed above may not be included in your school program but there is way more leniency in summer camps. There is no better time to educate your kids because they have the free time to ask questions as they learn more.

Innovative Learning is one of the first summer camps to offer a Bitcoin course to school-aged children in the United States. Based in Charlotte, NC, this summer camp aims to educate children *and* their parents on

Bitcoin and blockchain technology. The 3-week course will start July 29th, 2019 and features activities like Raspberry Pi mining, using a Bitcoin wallet, learning about a Blockchain and more! The founder, Belinda Colter is a black woman that should be celebrated for her innovation and faith in the Bitcoin community. Projects like this lay the groundwork for future generations to be educated at summer camps and programs around the world.

High School Students

As a former high school teacher, I understand that teenagers are always looking to learn about new technology. This generation of teens grew up with cell phones readily available so they will have no problem comprehending why Bitcoin is valuable to their generation. We have seen Bitcoin in popular magazines, movies, TV shows and posted on social media accounts.

Young black students are usually the product of the public-school system. The history of miseducation, lack of materials and underperforming test scores at public schools has plagued our community long enough. I propose that we petition school districts to implement courses about Bitcoin and Blockchain technology. Knowledge on this subject will expose kids to coding, advanced mathematics, international relations, economics, history and entrepreneurship. All students will benefit in the long run and principals along with school district leaders can be confident that students will be more desirable by colleges and jobs.

The subject of Bitcoin as a global payment system will force teenagers to realize the world around them.

Not only will knowledge empower them, but black students who have working knowledge about Bitcoin and blockchain can also enter any field or college with a head start on this emerging market. Numerous jobs are desperate to find people who can work for their blockchain company. We can flood the market with new, creative minds that can help build the future that we all want to see. Furthermore, since Bitcoin makes you inherently entrepreneurial, students who sell candy, shoes or videogames can start to accept Bitcoin instantly and join the community. Contact your local school superintendent and explain the need for your kids to learn about Bitcoin and blockchain technology.

If we cannot get these courses into schools for our children, then we must do the work ourselves. While high-school students are growing into adults we can help them enter the Bitcoin network. Give your kids allowance in cryptocurrency and show them how to send to friends for goods and services. Pay them with Bitcoin for small tasks like cutting grass or washing the car. We teach money management with balancing a checkbook, savings and giving to charity. These same concepts can be applied to Bitcoin and black students will benefit long-term.

Colleges and Universities

I'm glad to say that the skills needed to build a strong Bitcoin community can be used at Predominantly White Institutions (PWI) and Historically Black Colleges and Universities (HBCU). Students and administrators will need cooperation, but black students should lead the way. I propose that black students begin to start Bitcoin and blockchain groups, mine cryptocurrencies and request an option to pay for goods in Bitcoin.

Start a Campus Group!

The Howard University Blockchain Group is a great example of students who are passionate about building blockchain technology. Their influence has allowed students and local residents to learn more about this new innovation. Adoption can only happen when consumers are educated and motivated, therefore groups like these can plant the seed on campuses nationwide.

Groups that can properly educate other students should ask for funding from alumni who own Bitcoin. This is possible at any institution, but at HBCUs, most students are black and introducing our people as college students can spread adoption faster. I encourage black students at PWIs to do the same and if there is a group already started, join and invite others who believe they can learn about Bitcoin.

Schools such as Stanford, MIT and Princeton have developed online Bitcoin and blockchain courses. Their ability to educate students on and off campus has helped equipped thousands of young people with the tools to work in the new economy. The HBCUs that graduate majority of the black workforce should aim to offer similar Bitcoin and blockchain courses.

One example of a college-level Blockchain course is currently at Morgan State University. They recently partnered with Princeton University, Georgetown and 26 others to create the University Blockchain Research Initiative (UBRI). Following that partnership, they received funding from Ripple Labs to start a five-year partnership. Overall $50 Million dollars has been committed to the project and it will fund academic research, cryptocurrency, development and innovation in blockchain[33]. Pioneers like Ali Emdad and his staff should be celebrated in the black community for helping create programs like this. The next decade will see a wave of new blockchain-ready professionals in the black community and programs that mimic Morgan State will be celebrated.

Mine Cryptos

One of the perks of college is that students who live in the available housing make payments for their tuition, board and fees all at once. The amount of electricity they use is priced into the building so students essentially have free electricity. The process of mining cryptocurrencies is profitable for most coins over a long period of time, but the biggest expense is the cost of electricity. College students who live in dorms have the luxury of having free electricity.

Students can become the backbone of many crypto networks if you invest in mining software and hardware. Bitcoin mining has become too costly for most college students to make a profit but there are thousands of projects that need miners. Some use proof-of-work and others rely on proof-of-stake[34] but nonetheless mining can be profitable for black college students. Use that refund check for more than beer!

Students can also request that their Computer Science department allocate space to store cryptocurrency mining rigs. This can become a campus-wide project that uses the funds to pay for students' food, tuition or books. Even though you will have a large electricity cost, you will also have more space to assemble more mining rigs and ultimately earn more cryptocurrency. If a dedicated group of black students can start this project on HBCU or PWI campuses, they can be a beacon of light that shows the great use case of mining.

Crypto Payments

Publicly funded schools may have trouble offering a service that allows payments in Bitcoin, but private black colleges should aim to expand their international reach and accept Bitcoin. Students of all colors are growing up in a world where Bitcoin is used for payments. Why not become a visionary school and start to accept these payments for tuition? To take it a step further, why not allow Bitcoin payments at campus stores, sports events etc. Most HBCUs that are private tend to have financial troubles because of lack of interest. I propose that schools start the process of adding a Bitcoin payment option for tuition, books and fees.

Since Bitcoin is a global currency, the barrier for payment will no longer be a factor for lower-income international students. Perhaps they can receive school-sponsored loans with cryptocurrency used as collateral. We have seen this process work for projects like Maker DAO and their collateralized debt instruments. The payments are quick, seamless and smart contracts can be used instead of piles of paperwork. I will discuss more in a later chapter but solutions like this only help private institutions gain traction and pivot towards the right direction for the future.

Not only should private black colleges plan to accept Bitcoin for payments, but they should also invest in Bitcoin ATMs that allow students to buy and sell various cryptocurrencies. When you are looking to shape the minds of our next engineers, politicians and teachers you must provide a way for students to see the different options for joining the Bitcoin community. Bitcoin ATM kiosks can include different options such as a discount on fees for students. Furthermore, having a kiosk on-campus invites local residents to use the machine and raises profit margin for the school.

I am focusing on black college students at HBCUs because they graduate most of our current workforce, however, any black students at any college should petition their school to allow Bitcoin payments.

Professors

College professors who have a background in law, history, math or science should begin to equip themselves with knowledge about Bitcoin and blockchain technology. Most teachers will not need to use Bitcoin per se, but the implementation of blockchain technology across multiple disciplines is inevitable. Learning how this new technology will impact your field can lead to new positions, community awards and a legacy of innovation.

For example, Professor Tonya Evans of New Hampshire School of Law teaches about the intersection of blockchain and law. Evans also created the Cryptocurrency & Law online professional certificate program. Recently, Evans won the Enterprise Blockchain Leadership Award for her work. This is another shining

example of the potential to impact your field by
introducing blockchain technology.

Endowment Funds

Recently Harvard, Stanford, MIT and other
schools made their first investment into a cryptocurrency
fund with their multi-billion-dollar endowment[35]. These
schools have committed tens of millions of dollars to
invest in cryptocurrency funds and blockchain-based
companies. These funds will receive equity in
blockchain-based companies as well as exposure to
physical cryptocurrencies. Even though their exposure is
small, investment from institutional endowments with
more than $39.2 Billion further legitimizes the space.

I propose that Historically Black Colleges and

Universities make a similar choice and allocate a portion of their endowment money to cryptocurrency funds. According to a Bloomberg analysis, no school with more than a $1 Billion endowment fund was an HBCU, with Howard coming in first at $578 Million. "Wealth begets more wealth" is the old saying and it looks like these institutions can see where the future wealth will be coming from. Alumni and future alumni should contact their respective schools and have cryptocurrency as a part of their endowment fund investment. It is still early in the game and we have to develop a sense of urgency about adoption and investment into the next asset class for the future.

At every level we have to do our part to first, educate ourselves and second, educate our children on Bitcoin and blockchain technology. This is an exciting time in world history, and we get to say we lived during the first great financial shift in 100 years. Passing down this valuable information will have an impact on all future generations, and we have to start the work today!

CHAPTER 4 | BUCK THE FANKS

On the heels of the second bailout for London banks, the Bitcoin whitepaper was released in 2008. The creator of the world's first cryptocurrency made it very clear that Bitcoin was invented to make sure banks would not have too much power in the future. Nakamoto wanted to make sure people around the world could avoid the tyranny of the banking system and purchase goods between two parties without their help as a third party. Most adults can remember the financial collapse of 2008 and the downturn of the real estate market. If you don't remember why, here is a quick recap:

1. June 2003, the Fed lowers interest rates down to 1%, the lowest in 45 years.

2. October 2004, SEC lowered the net capital requirements for five banks including Goldman Sachs, Merrill Lynch, Lehman Brothers, Bear Stearns and Morgan Stanley. This allowed riskier investment and the introduction of sub-prime loans at a higher rate.

3. Late 2004, home ownership reached 70% but the interest rates hiked to 5.25%, leaving many people unable to make payments

4. August 2007, the liquidity problem began stretching outside borders as Northern Rock in Britain had to request funding from the Bank of England

5. Late 2007, Merrill Lynch was sold to Bank of America, Bear Stearns acquired by JP Morgan and

Lehman Brothers filed for bankruptcy

6. Troubled Assets Relief Program (TARP) puts the total bailout numbers at $700 Billion but according to Mother Jones publication the total number is closer to $14.4 Trillion[36].

Following this recession many people begin to question their government-backed currency for the first time. The term "too big to fail" was a perfect description of the big banks who mishandled our pensions, retirement funds and housing loans. Money had become too centralized which bred corruption and greed.

Citizens of all ethnicities and backgrounds were affected, but let's take a step back and look at how the black community has been disregarded by various banks over a long period of time. The Guardian released a story in 2015 showing how "redlining" has affected the black community before the housing crisis of 2008. The Housing and Urban Development (HUD) report states that "Borrowers in upper-income black neighborhoods were twice as likely as homeowners in low-income white neighborhoods to refinance with a subprime loan.[37]"

Stories of fighting an uphill battle with banks for a housing loan have been discussed by black people for decades. For most families, their wealth comes from homeownership or home equity. Since this right was systematically withheld from most black people in the 1930s and the practice continues today, then we have to find a solution to take power away from large banks. Here are just a few examples of racially charged acts by some of the largest banks in America:

JP Morgan

"JP Morgan Settles Racist Loans Claims with $55 million payment" (Jan. 2017)

An African-American taking out a $191,100 loan on average paid $1,126 more over the first five years of the loan than a white borrower.

Bank of America

"BofA/Countrywide to pay $335 Million for predatory lending" (Dec. 2011)

Following the purchase of Countrywide, Bank of America had to foot the bill for this settlement which showed that over 200,000 loans made to blacks and Latinos were steered towards subprime loans even with

BITCOIN AND BLACK AMERICA

equal qualifications.

Bank of America

"BofA Fined $2M for Racial Discrimination" (Sep. 2013)

The presiding judge, Linda Chapman, found that "the bank applied unfair and inconsistent selection criteria resulting in the rejection of qualified African-American applicants for teller and entry-level clerical and administrative positions."

Merrill Lynch

"Merrill Lynch $160 Million Racial Bias Settlement" (Aug. 2013)

This suit was brought about by black brokers who were dismissed as "poor performers" even though most of their white clients would not accept them based on race.

Wells Fargo

"$175 Million for racist lending practice" (July 2012)

Wells Fargo was found guilty for making over 30,000 black and Latino applicants pay a higher mortgage or accept subprime loans even with equal qualifications as their white counterparts.

The Black community doesn't owe the banking system anything.

If you work for a bank, unfortunately, I have to flame your profession, but the truth is easy to see. You can love your job and use your talent to prosper in your career. More power to you. Or you can develop a plan to exit the banking field and use your talents at a top blockchain company or cryptocurrency project. Many projects need the brilliant financial minds of the banking sector to make blockchain technology usable for mainstream consumers. Software developers and programmers dominate the Bitcoin industry, but black people in the banking industry can take financial roles to help with the business side of the project. One common theme among cryptocurrency projects is great technology, terrible financial sense. Auditors, accountants, loan officers and tellers can find a place in the blockchain industry. I am confident that black people can use the next decade to at least consider using their powers for good instead of helping the same institutions that keep us enslaved.

We have already seen examples of top executives leaving banking positions for the blockchain industry. For example, Christopher Matta was named Vice President of Goldman Sachs and two days later he left[38]. His six years of working there didn't matter. The CEO of Goldman Sachs calling him crazy didn't matter. The realization of where the financial industry is moving is what mattered. Now, Matta is the Co-Founder at Crescent Crypto Asset Management based in New York.

Amber Baldet is another example of a high-ranking banker leaving that sector for a blockchain company. She is the former head of JP Morgan's blockchain and smart contract unit. A few weeks in she probably realized that working on a centralized bank coin with a private blockchain was not fulfilling. Baldet left to start her own company Clovyr[39], which is a decentralized platform for building blockchain applications. The examples are there for black bankers to follow, so if you would rather help build the future than uphold the past, join the Bitcoin and blockchain sector as a professional.

Not only are we affected by the inflation caused by stagnant wages and growing prices, but we also have constant reminders that the banking system has no regard for the black community. We have to stop trying to appeal to the moral authority of these institutions who obviously have no morals when it comes to doing business with our community.

Protests such as "Occupy Wall Street" did not work. A bunch of disgruntled citizens sleeping in tents and playing banjos outside of a bank achieves nothing in regard to social change. In addition, black men and women who join these protests are more likely to be arrested and physically subdued by police. I don't believe that putting your life on the line for a weak protest that achieves nothing will work for the black community. Furthermore, I don't think it's a smart decision to physically harm bankers or their co-conspirators. Most black people I know are not going to start physically harming people who have systematically taken wealth out of our community.

I propose that we build our foundation of social change and protest by steadily moving our funds out of the banking system. The only way to hurt the banks is to disrupt their cash flow and profits. I understand that Bitcoin and cryptocurrency cannot be regarded as a completely reliable medium of exchange and unit of account at this current state, but it can absolutely be used as a store of value for the long-term.

Slowly moving funds from your retirement or savings into Bitcoin or cryptocurrency has proven profitable over the past eight years. Past performance does not always indicate future success but when given the options, this is our best option to both grow our wealth and systematically make banks understand that we will not stand for this discrimination. Banks like JP Morgan Chase, Bank of America and Wells Fargo have begun charging a monthly fee to store your money, charge you an overdraft fee for being too poor[40] and still use an outdated system of fees and time to process wire transfers. These actions along with the information provided before should light a fire inside of you that will help you plan your exit from the banking system.

If you think about fiat currency, the only reason it

has value is because you are told it has value. Forced

consensus. No matter the scenario, you are losing money

by keeping it stored in a bank savings account. If you

keep your money in a savings account and assume, we

keep a 2.5% inflation rate, in 40 years:

$1 spent is $0

$1 stored is 37cents. A loss of 63% in value.

$1 saved at the bank earning 2.3% is 92 cents, a loss of

8%

Furthermore, most American banks practice

fractional reserve banking. This means that they only

have to keep a portion of their net worth in cash held in a

vault. According to Wonderopolis[41], banks with $15.2

million to $110.2 million in transaction accounts must hold 3% in reserve. Large banks (those with more than $110.2 million in transaction accounts) must hold 10% in reserve. This means that you are using digital currency that is processed using their own ledger technology. If there was ever an economic crisis, like in Greece, most banks would be unable to stay open due to bank runs for customers who want cash. At the very least, having Bitcoin and cryptocurrency as a "Plan B" should be an option for all black people in America.

Banks are a long-standing institution and it would be preposterous to suggest that all black people stop using banks completely at this time. Most of our mortgages, loans and direct deposits depend on the banking system currently. I suggest that if we have to use banks, take your business to black-owned credit unions or banks that benefit the black community. If the customers of these banks begin to request that Bitcoin payments to exchanges like Coinbase and Uphold are considered, we can have a seamless onboarding process. There are over 35 black-owned credit unions in the U.S. such as Mechanics and Farmers in Durham, NC and One United Bank[42].

These credit unions should begin to accept blockchain-based companies for business accounts. Opening up black-owned banks to these new companies will bring in fresh capital from around the US and lead to more capital for lending and investment. Silvergate Bank, based in San Diego, CA, has over 500 digital currency-related clients and is growing steadily. They have companies, miners and developers using their bank and they account for 11.3% of their total customer base. They took advantage of other banks being scared to accept these companies and have made $8.3 billion in investment since 2013[43].

Billions of dollars in fresh capital is available to black-owned credit unions if they are proactive and plan for the inevitable. With news about projects like the JP Morgan coin, partnerships between banks and crypto companies are inevitable. Our community deserves to be at the forefront of the next financial revolution. We can achieve another self-fulfilling prophecy. Accept blockchain-based business deposits, which leads to increased funding for housing, education and businesses, then finally, more capital for our community as a whole. Although the vision of Bitcoin and cryptocurrency is to create a new financial system, we have to bridge the gap until that day comes.

CHAPTER 5 INTERNATIONAL COOPERATION

The black community in America is the focus of much of this book, but we are not a monolithic group. Black people from all parts of the world will participate in building the Bitcoin and cryptocurrency community. Citizens from African nations, the Caribbean, Europe and others have also been exposed to many of the problems facing the black American community. Many immigrants and their children still have to deal with our inability to form an economic foundation that benefits the black population.

One of the ways we can use Bitcoin and cryptocurrency to promote international cooperation is for remittance payments. Numerous families have to send money back home and vice versa. Most of the current businesses like MoneyGram and Western Union have exorbitant fees and wait times associated with these payments. If black Americans do our part to start circulating the "black dollar" via cryptocurrency we can establish an infrastructure that allows payments to family and friends abroad.

This will not be an easy process due to different economic policies and technological infrastructure. When you send 1 Bitcoin, the process for using that Bitcoin for payment or selling it for fiat currency is a long and tough process. However, demand for these services coupled with increased development will make these payments seamless in the future. Having a reliable Bitcoin ATM in the country where you send payments is a good first step. Having an online exchange that can help transfers happen instantly is another good step in the right direction.

Cryptocurrency Projects around the Globe

Currently we have companies like BitMari, founded by Sinclair Skinner, that allows payments to citizens in Zimbabwe via Bitcoin. Projects like these should be supported by our community and show an example of how we can provide a solution for black people abroad to receive money without using a high-cost third party. As the primary use case for Bitcoin changes from a store of value to a medium of exchange, we can have the tools in place to facilitate these transactions.

BitPesa is another company that allows payments to citizens of Tanzania, Uganda, Nigeria, DRC, Senegal, Ghana and Morocco that are faster and cheaper than traditional methods. They state that their cost of business is 1-3% compared to 10% from other companies. The process takes 1-24 hours compared to a few days by other methods. Luno is another company that is available to Nigerian and South African citizens who want to receive Bitcoin or Ethereum instead of traditional fiat currencies.

In the Dominican Republic they have the crypto exchange, Coin Field. They are one of the top ten countries for remittance payments in cryptocurrency[44]. Their government has used a hands-off policy thus far in regard to regulation and that has allowed the industry to flourish. In Barbados, Gabriel Abed founded the Bitcoin exchange, Bitt. His work to bring awareness about cryptocurrency to the Bermuda government is another example of how we can have international solutions with a focus on the local economy.

Jamaica has been in the news lately due to their announcement that they will use the Jamaican Stock Exchange to pilot Bitcoin and Ethereum trades[45]. The regulation put out by their government is similar to other countries who don't recognize "virtual currency" as a regulated currency. However, they have validated these cryptocurrencies as an emerging asset class that can be purchased and stored in a secure and regulatory environment.

Reggie Middleton, the creator of Veritaseum, has done significant work with Jamaican financial regulators to help bring blockchain solutions in the capital markets.

His project allows legacy institutions to benefit from digital asset trading by issuing the Veritas token and initiating P2P transactions.

Alakanani Itireleng has used Bitcoin donations to grow food and provide groceries for families in her native country, Botswana. She is also the CEO of the Satoshi Centre which is a blockchain tech hub. Her contributions to the cryptocurrency space have helped spread awareness and is a perfect example of how we can use digital assets abroad.

Many young professionals in America have a background from an immigrant family. A lot of our talented people are paid handsomely to work for a large company that will ultimately only benefit the company. However, if we can use our collective brain power to build blockchain applications that positively affect our people around the world, we can start to see changes. Problems like healthcare, voting, basic human rights and war are not problems that can be solved overnight but we must use what we have to get what we want.

Projects such as Akoin address this issue and can help build cryptocurrency ecosystems in the African diaspora[46]. This project was the idea of the five-time Grammy nominated singer and philanthropist, Akon. In the recent Newsweek article, they state, "Akoin would provide a platform for entrepreneurs to create, market and monetize their own decentralized applications, or Dapps. His cryptocurrency could surmount a key challenge for doing business in a fragmented economy: 54 currencies for 54 nations. [47]" The tech needed to provide services in various countries will be built using blockchain technology and funded using cryptocurrency.

People like Akon and his supporters realize the future is here and can, as he states, "bring power back to the people."

This announcement came on the heels of his "Lighting Africa" project which will provide a reliable solar grid for power in distressed areas. The synergy of these ideas coupled with the location of the project should make you realize that the future of commerce and growth will involve African nations. The bridge between our homeland may not be physical, but in 2019, we have the ability to connect with like-minded individuals through financial technology like Bitcoin.

CHAPTER 6 | FUTURE SOLUTIONS

Ten years ago, Bitcoin and blockchain technology emerged on to the world stage. Most people could not have predicted that early forum talks, and online communities would evolve into a $300 Billion-dollar industry. Since the first block was mined, developers, economists, speculators and users have built solutions for this economy. The first problem was onboarding new users and we saw centralized exchanges like Coinbase and Gemini solve that issue. Accessibility via the phone became easier with the emergence of Cash App and Abra. The introduction of KYC/AML laws brought about the need for decentralized exchanges (DEX) where you can use technology like atomic swaps and smart contracts to trade digital assets. Scalability for global payments was another issue that is being solved with the advancement of the Lightning Network and off-chain payments. All of these solutions were once "future" solutions and today they have been seamlessly integrated into the Bitcoin industry.

The global black community should join in this process and provide future solutions. Now that we know Bitcoin, blockchain technology and cryptocurrency are not going away, we should start to use these tools to solve social problems or at the very least address the problem in a new way. Different aspects of everyday life like politics, music, sports and religion can all be impacted by this new industry. We will have to make a concerted effort to push these solutions forward and change the way things have been done in all aspects of our social life.

Blockchain Politics

South Korean conservative party LKP, has launched a blockchain-based political party[48]. They are implementing blockchain technology in four major areas:

1.   Record meeting results of the central and local parties' assemblies

2.   Record and evaluate the key performance of members' activities

3.   Voting process for elections in the party, online system and transparency

4.   Petition system, prevent fraud and manipulation

These new processes lay the groundwork for a more transparent and honest political system. The black community is not a monolithic group and our politics are diverse. However, we should leverage our voice to require that blockchain technology needs to be implemented into any party that wants our support. No matter your affiliation, black voters in the national, state and local levels should demand a higher level of transparency and trust from elected officials.

Projects like Coin Center advocate for blockchain technology at the national level and many Bitcoin and cryptocurrency groups advocate for adoption at the state and local level. If the black American community can begin to join these groups and contact politicians, we may start to see a shift in the political world. The most important aspect of politics is money. Let's face it, whoever can raise the most money will usually win the political race. No broke boys allowed in the political game. Donations to politicians have traditionally been fiat based, but recently a new wave of elected officials and candidates began accepting Bitcoin for donation[49]. The list includes:

Greg Abbott	Governor	Texas
Bob Barr	Candidate for US Representative	Georgia
Rand Paul	Senator	Kentucky
Steve Stockman	Candidate for Senator	Texas
Gavin Newsom	Governor	California
Paul Dietzel	Candidate for US Representative	Louisiana
Bryan Parker	Candidate for Mayor	Oakland, CA
Will Hammer	Candidate for US Representative	Virginia
Jared Polis	Governor	Colorado

The only drawbacks are that states such as California and Kansas have banned these practices. Also, bitcoin contributions are capped at $100, much lower than the $2,700 max on presidential campaigns. The future of political donations to black politicians using bitcoin could open our options up to a broader base that will only grow in the future. The list above featured only one black politician, but hopefully after reading this book, others will be compelled to accept Bitcoin as well.

Over time, if we adopt the principles of a 21st century economy, store wealth in Bitcoin and circulate our dollars via cryptocurrency we will have a head start on funding honest and transparent politicians. We have to demand that we have blockchain processes in our chosen political parties and the option to donate in Bitcoin.

Music

During the age of streaming and music apps, there has never been a better time for black musicians to capitalize on their value and popularity. The only problem is that popular streaming apps such as Apple Music and Spotify know this as well and leverage that into paying less than a penny per stream to the musical artist[50].

Platforms such as Soundcloud allow musicians to directly upload content for listeners and this is a step in the right direction. However, owning your masters and being able to make a profit from music sales has long been a problem in our community. Even though black people invented rock and roll, jazz, house music, R&B and hip-hop music, we have yet to take control of the industry because most artists are paid crumbs in exchange for popularity. I commend Jay-Z for creating Tidal and offering to pay more to artists than other platforms. In the future, blockchain technology could replace this model and put the power back into the hands of the artist.

Imagine a future where artists can upload content to a platform and the "profit-sharing" is governed by math instead of human greed. Companies like, Ujo Music, have taken the charge and plan to "liberate music" with their platform. This type of platform would allow artists to receive cryptocurrency payment from users, and the middleman cost that is inflated by these companies will be substantially lower. Low fees and a decentralized market allow musicians to provide music directly to the source, own their masters and allow users to pay based on what they play.

There are other solutions to this problem being built and new advancements like micropayments are becoming the new type of profit model. Micropayments allow a user to "pay as you go" as opposed to a rigid monthly cost where it doesn't matter if you listened to 1 song or 1000 songs. Companies like Resonate have implemented micropayments into their platform and realize that the current streaming model is broken. I propose that black artists seek out new companies such as these to leverage our power as the driving force of the industry. I realize many artists are contractually obligated to make music for major labels, but young black kids have to be taught a different way. Blockchain technology in music can be that solution in the future.

The technology behind streaming platforms will take time to be mainstream and user-friendly, however, musicians are accepting cryptocurrency payments for music right now. 50 Cent accepted bitcoins in exchange for his 2014 album *Animal Ambition* and earned over 700 bitcoins[51]. At the time it was worth several hundred thousand, but when the story came out his bitcoin holdings were worth $7.7 million. This is a good example of a popular musician using Bitcoin to increase his profit and also receive free promotion. What more could young black musicians want than an increase in value over time and free promotion? This is possible when you accept cryptocurrency for payments.

Artists such as Kanye West, Nas, Childish Gambino, Migos, and Future have all publicly stated that they own a few bitcoins. Soulja Boy actually made a song entitled "Bitcoin" in 2018. Musicians such as Larry June and Big Sean have also mentioned Bitcoin or cryptocurrency on new songs. A lot of black musicians are starting to wake up and realize what the future holds for financial policy. If we can do our part to introduce this option to the new generation of musicians, we can have a huge stake in how the music business operates in the future.

Sports

According to 2015 statistics, black athletes make up 77% of the National Basketball Association (NBA) and over 68% of the National Football League (NFL). Contracts with these teams and endorsement deals with other companies such as Nike have pushed the black athlete to the forefront of American sports. Some of the most visible faces of the black community participate in these leagues and we should establish economic leverage via Bitcoin and cryptocurrency. Athletes who get drafted or signed to these teams should start to ask that a percentage of their salary or endorsement deal be paid in Bitcoin. This is another example of the "self-fulfilling prophecy" that is described in Chapter 2.

If black athletes start the conversation about being paid in Bitcoin and cryptocurrency, major companies will have to adjust their business model to compensate for paying these athletes. What does that do? It forces them to constantly buy, hold and use bitcoin. This drives market demand, leading to mainstream trust and purchase of bitcoins for themselves. Two-time Pro Bowler and Super Bowl champion, Russell Okung has already started this trend and famously asked owners to "pay me in Bitcoin." According to him he personally knows over 30 NFL players who have dipped a toe in the Bitcoin market. I am sure this number will increase drastically over the next few years. Demand coupled with a scarce supply drives the fundamental price and those athletes who decide to get paid in Bitcoin will actually have *more* value added to their brand.

I am not suggesting that athletes go all-in on using Bitcoin, but a nuanced approach can definitely be achieved. For example, Spencer Dinwiddie of the New Jersey Nets started his own shoe line named "K8IROS". He has enabled fans to purchase these shoes using fiat currency as well as Bitcoin. Instead of receiving his salary in Bitcoin, he provided a product where he could *earn* Bitcoin. Like I discussed in Chapter 2, in the 21st century economy, selling goods for Bitcoin is the easiest way to accumulate or as the cool kids call it "stacking sats.[52]" Other athletes can follow Dinwiddie's example and sell their own merchandise for Bitcoin.

The NFLPA has also entered the blockchain space with an investment in SportsCastr[53]. This blockchain-based platform allows fans to view NFL games with their choice of commentary. When you create content, you are rewarded with tokens that can be used later to purchase goods. There are many decentralized projects being built and the NFL recognizes that this is the technology of the future.

In the NBA, the Sacramento Kings have begun mining Ethereum for a new charitable program called "Mining for Good"[54]. They are installing mining machines in their data facility and will become the first professional team to mine cryptocurrency. The Kings also made waves by becoming the first professional team to accept Bitcoin for payments[55]. In 2014, the Kings sent shockwaves around the world with this announcement. Through a partnership with BitPay, they were able to provide another payment option.

The Black Church

Over the last 400 years in America, the black church has been a staple of the black community. The church has been a financial epicenter and social network that has stood the test of time. Every Sunday millions of black people attend these services for their spiritual nourishment. The words of the pastor, encouragement from parishioners and the sense of community make the black church a delightful place to gather. There is no other institution in the world that can gather millions of black people with different political and social views for a few hours each week. If we truly want to integrate

Bitcoin into our community, every black church, mosque or religious gathering in America needs to accept bitcoins for tithes and offering.

Non-profit organizations with "501c3" listings can currently accept Bitcoin for donation. Right now. This is not some voodoo that will take years to establish, we can do this right now. As a matter of fact, I'm sure there is a deacon or pastor for someone's church reading right now. You can print the QR code from a Bitcoin wallet on the tithing envelopes, the church website or the back of the fans with MLK Jr.'s face.

You have many options to make this shift in payment methods happen. I know a lot of ministries have taken the step to accept digital donations online or via phone applications. The natural next step is to accept Bitcoin and cryptocurrency. Much like the Catholic church stores some of its wealth in gold, if a large portion of black churches can start to store a small percentage of their holdings in Bitcoin, we can own a good portion of the best money system in the world. The war chest needed to keep black churches funded will benefit from adding Bitcoin and cryptocurrency.

Patrons can take steps to educate themselves on Bitcoin and other cryptocurrencies. Bills that require fiat payments will still have to be paid, so partnerships with businesses like BitRefill or Uphold can give our black churches a choice to sell some Bitcoin and hold a percentage for the future.

Peer to Peer Loans

Companies like Coin Loan allow people who are seeking loans to use their digital assets as collateral for a cash loan. We explored the pitfalls of getting a loan from a bank for a lot of black applicants in Chapter 4, so we have to use other options in the future. Coin Loan is just one of many companies who are looking at the future value of crypto assets and are willing to trade fiat currency for these assets. Everyone has their own use case for cryptocurrency and for those who don't want to HODL, this is an option to leverage your assets for fiat currency. These loans can be used for purchases and provide a way for early crypto investors to enter the financial market without a credit check or discrimination.

Maker DAO is another project that seeks to provide loans in a similar way. They have a

Collateralized Debt Position (CDP) available for Ethereum users. If you purchase Ethereum assets today and use them as collateral for a loan, Maker DAO has a smart contract that can complete that process. This project also curtails unnecessary credit checks and simply uses what you own to get what you want. If you start to accumulate digital assets today, in the future you can use a CDP to borrow money and purchase real estate and other assets without surrendering your digital assets. This can be a win-win for the black community in America and abroad because it provides an option free of bias.

Central Backed Digital Currency

Also known as CBDCs, these digital currencies are created by various governments to make the financial system completely digital. Not to be confused with cryptocurrency, these coins do not operate on a public blockchain, but rather, on the same private ledger that has operated before. Blockchain technology will make cross-border payments secure and cheaper for large institutions. However, for the everyday person, these currencies are not needed and will most likely be forced upon most populations.

JP Morgan announced their successful test of a digital coin in February 2019 with the JPM Coin. Next, we saw the huge announcement from Facebook that they would be creating their own "cryptocurrency" called Libra. This project aims to introduce millions of unbanked citizens to digital money. These coins are both different forms of CBDCs and will most likely be used to onboard new users.

Grow Food. Mine Cryptocurrency.

Brucy Hardy is an entrepreneur from Canada who builds sustainable food systems. His hobby of mining Bitcoin led to him developing a process for using excess heat from Bitcoin miners to grow food. Anyone who has mined cryptocurrency will have to deal with noise from fans and heat generated from the computers running 24/7. In your personal home the sound and extra heat are annoying, but when paired with a greenhouse, can make growing food more efficient.

He has set up a system that takes the excess heat from the mining machines and allows for flexibility in growing plants such as fresh lettuce. Since he is in a colder environment, the heat also helps with keeping the house warm and allows him to profit from mining while growing his own food supply.

His example should be used by the black community to better our future. Money is important but it doesn't matter without a healthy community. The increase in awareness about our food supply has started a renaissance of farmers in the black community[56]. We should use this time period of growth to introduce cryptocurrency mining as well. Kill two birds with one stone. Make money from electricity and grow healthy food options. This process can easily be duplicated and taught to interested consumers. This is another example of how we can use cryptocurrency to create a sustainable future.

Security Token Offering (STO)

Companies looking to raise capital have traditionally used VC investment and crowdfunding. The cryptocurrency market took this idea to another level and introduced Initial Coin Offerings (ICOs). These "coin offerings" allow a business to post their whitepaper and roadmap for production. They offer coins at a fixed price to investors and once the funding round ends, these investors are rewarded with these digital coins. The value of these coins fluctuates based on market sentiment and many people between 2015 and 2017 used these offerings to enrich themselves. The process is easy and seamless, but the SEC regarded these coins as "securities" due to its adherence to the Howey Test. This led to a dramatic decrease in ICOs funding and ushered in a new era of fundraising called Security Token Offerings (STOs).

STOs allow business owners to register with the SEC and offer coins to investors. Since the value of these coins can increase over time due to fundamentals or company success, these offerings are treated as securities. The biggest issue in the black community, in regard to entrepreneurship, is access to capital. This new fundraising technique opens up a new way of investment and takes away the barriers previously set before. You do not have to be an accredited investor and the minimum investment amount is much lower than traditional methods.

Dawn Dickson just finished the first STO for a black-owned company in history. She raised over $1 million dollars from 2,117 investors[57]. The company she founded, PopCom, provides software for customer data, and kiosks for businesses called a PopShop. We should applaud her efforts while looking to create companies that utilize this new tool for raising capital.

Crypto Meetups and Lounges

Bitcoin was birthed online but the community stays engaged with meetups and centers that focus on education. Many of the meetups I have attended included speakers from different disciplines and gives novices a chance to network with people in the industry. As more people begin to adopt Bitcoin and learn about blockchain technology there will be many opportunities to hold meetups in your respective city.

One company in Inglewood, CA has taken this approach by creating the Crypto Blockchain Plug center. This black-owned center offers large conference rooms, meeting rooms, free coffee and WiFi to anyone who becomes a member. A "crypto-workspace" is the best way to educate newbies and connect crypto entrepreneurs around the city. The owners, Jaci Marie and Najah

Roberts, are a perfect example of people from our community leveraging cryptocurrency to have classes, meetups and events such as the popular, Wine, Women and Crypto series.

Virtual reality meetups are an extremely new concept, but the first Bitcoin VR meetup happened in April 2019. The high cost of blockchain conferences have become an issue and VR meetups will make it much cheaper to hold a meeting of the minds. This idea is on the ground floor but if the black community wants to have a global impact, we have to start looking at this type of solution. Guest speakers, networking and even music breaks can make these events fun and convenient because you don't have to leave your home.

Personally, I prefer meeting in person, but the next generation will rely on VR technology much more in the future. We can move ahead of schedule and have these

platforms set up for members of the black community and

future generations

CHAPTER 7 | BLACKCHAIN

It would be a waste of time to write this entire

book urging black people to invest in Bitcoin without

working on a solution that uses Bitcoin. Black business

owners received less than 1% of the money invested by

venture capitalists in 2017. Black women are awarded

even less funding, only receiving 0.2% of all startup

funds[58]. The Blackchain web application will solve this

problem by matching black business owners with

investors around the world.

This platform will give black business owners the

visibility, education and money needed to start a successful business. We do not discriminate on the Blackchain platform, but we will focus on making sure that black ownership is at the forefront and black investors can have top talent available on one platform.

Blackchain is an open source project for peer-to-peer loans and equity crowdfunding. Fiat currency will be the dominant form of money used for investment but an option to use Bitcoin will be available. Some businesses do not need funding right now but rather, more support from customers, so we will have an expansive directory as well.

The credentials needed to receive investment are governed by a "social credit score." This score allows entrepreneurs to submit information about their business and become more visible to investors. Information such as your EIN number, cash flow, employees, and business sector decrease the risk associated with using Bitcoin to invest in a business. Moreover, global investment is possible because there are no barriers on Bitcoin or altcoins.

Lastly, the process to become a founder, incorporate your business and become profitable can be challenging. We will assist business owners by providing an education portal to bring them up to speed on the funding process. All of these features will be available on the web application and currently we have the private beta version available for select users who have signed up on the website.

The Blackchain syndicate fund will use the web application as a direct pipeline for investors to support businesses. The fund will be formed in December 2019 and businesses who use the Blackchain app will be eligible for investment. Not only do we aim to use cryptocurrency as the primary source of funding, but we will also use blockchain technology to ensure transparency and a voting system that allows all investors to choose which businesses will receive funds. This fund is in development now and will be flexible enough to fund brick and mortar stores, tech startups, blockchain companies and even opportunity zones.

Opportunity Zones

According to the Economic Innovation Group, opportunity zones "provides a series of incentives to unlock capital gains for investment into underserved communities across the country." These "underserved" communities are statistically filled with black people.

Therefore, we should make every effort to make sure that investment in these communities includes black people and black businesses. If not, we will start to see rampant gentrification in historically black neighborhoods. We live in a capitalist society so the pursuit of property is open to all, but we have to leverage our money and resources to make sure we can own the neighborhoods that we call home.

Opportunity zones allow investors to do three things:

1. A temporary deferral: An investor can defer capital gains taxes until 2026 by rolling their gains directly over into an Opportunity Fund.

2.   A reduction: The deferred capital gains liability is effectively reduced by 10% if the investment in the Opportunity Fund is held for 5 years and another 5% if held for 7 years.

3.   An exemption: Any capital gains on subsequent investments made through an Opportunity Fund accrue tax-free as long as the investor stays invested in the fund for at least 10 years.

These perks will produce a windfall of money to be made by investors over the next decade. The Blackchain project is introducing the syndicate fund so that investors can use fiat or crypto to start an "opportunity fund". This fund will be a subsidiary of the overall fund due to regulations, but if we can begin raising capital this year, there is no reason why we can't take advantage of the tax benefits and exemptions presented above.

Support the Blackchain Project

We are still in the early stages of development but if you would like to join this project, invest in the syndicate fund, or invest in black-owned businesses, visit the website[59].

I want to make sure that I accompany this book with actual solutions to the problems we are experiencing in this country and abroad. The days of being a victim and waiting for others to help us are over. If you agree, join us in building a prosperous future with Blackchain.

BLACK BLOCKCHAIN DIRECTORY

The following people are black leaders in the Bitcoin and blockchain industry. Take some time to reach out to these people and help build a solid network for the future.

www.bitcoinandblackamerica.com

Gabriel Abed

Founder & CEO, Bitt

Barbados

Michael Abraha

Blockchain Business Development, 500 BC Foundry

Baltimore, MD

Victor Akoma-Phillips

COO, KuBitX Exchange

Calgary, Alberta, Canada

Shannon Allen

CIO, Cryptic Coin

Miami, FL

Joshua Armah

Blockchain Craftsmanship

San Francisco, CA

Adewale Bankole

The Bastiat Society

Nigeria

Chris Bates

Bitland Global

Bloomington, IN

King Bless

KRBE Digital Assets Group

Los Angeles, CA

Crypto Blood

The Crypto Blood Show

Detroit, MI

Kevin Boyette

Owner, Presto Bitcoin

Washington D.C.

Joel Braithwaite

Braithwaite Legal, LLC

Washington D.C.

Tongayi Choto

Product Development

Zimbabwe

Kelauni Cook

Co-Founder, Distributed49

Pittsburgh, PA

Tavonia Evans

Founder, GUAP Coin

Atlanta, GA

Tonya Evans

UNH Blockchain Law

Boston, MA

Ariana Fowler

Lead PM, ConSensys

Brooklyn, NY

Magdeldin Hamid

ConSensys

Washington D.C.

Arthur Hayes

CEO, BitMEX

Seychelles

Alexia Hefti

Blockchain Tax Lead, Deloitte

Canada

M'Bwebe Ishangi

Blackchain Mining Group

Brooklyn, NY

Alakanani Itireleng

Director, Satoshi Centre

Botswana

Christian Kakoba

Community Lead, BitHub Africa

Kenya

John Karanja

Founder, BitHub Africa

Kenya

Eden Kidane

Blockchain Project Manager, Hello Tractor

Kenya

Daniel Kimotho

Co-founder, EOS Nairobi

Kenya

Ingrid LaFleur

Chief Community Officer, EOS Detroit

Detroit, MI

Ashonzay Matlock

CEO, ZayToken Coaching Services

Washington D.C.

Deidre McIntyre

Founder, Black People and Cryptocurrency

Facebook Group

Reggie Middleton

CEO, Veritaseum

New York, NY

Maureen Murat, Esq.

Crowdie Advisors, LLC

Washington D.C.

Lianna Newman

Developer, ConSensys

Washington, D.C.

Pascal Ntsama IV

Coincentrix Capital

Atlanta, GA

Olayinka Odeniran

Managing Director, Black Women Blockchain Council

Maryland

Daisy Ozim

Director, Blockchain for Social Justice

San Francisco, CA

Troy Pelshak

Senior PM, Atlas Zen LLC

Charlotte, NC

Jomari Peterson

CEO, The Digital Reserve

San Francisco, CA

Justin Rhedrick

CEO, Bitcoin Vegan LLC

Charlotte, NC

Kwame Rugunda

Africa Blockchain Conference

Uganda

Talisha Shine

Consultant, Blockchain Consortium International

Washington, D.C.

Sinclair Skinner

BitMari

Zimbabwe/Washington D.C.

Evander Smart

Founder, Bitcoin University

Miami, FL

Mamadou Kwidjim Toure

Founder, Ubuntu Capital Group

Ivory Coast

Samson Williams

Partner, Axes and Eggs

Washington D.C.

Lamar Wilson

Founder, Wacoinda

Kentucky

REFERENCES

[1] North Carolina.

https://www.usatoday.com/story/money/careers/2018/05/16/states-where-teachers-paid-most-and-least/34964975/

[2] The first popular P2P exchange that allowed Bitcoin payments. Shut down in 2014.

[3] Mark Karpeles-owned exchange that shut down in 2014 due to liquidity problems

[4] Denomination of Bitcoin. 1 Million satoshis = 1 Bitcoin.

[5] Fear, uncertainty and doubt

[6] Hold on for Dear Life

[7] Facebook Project aiming to bring a centralized digital currency to Facebook users. Subsidiary company is Calibra.

[8] Computing power being used as "work" to validate network

[9] Contracts that are digitally signed and secured based on software and cryptography

[10] RIP Hal Finney. Cryptographer, father and first person to receive bitcoins.

[11] Fixed, hexadecimal number that allows for large data set to be encrypted

[12] https://bitnodes.earn.com/

[13] The Racial Wealth Gap Is Leading to An Almost-Nonexistent Middle Class

https://www.commondreams.org/news/2017/09/13/racial-wealth-gap-leading-almost-nonexistent-middle-class

[14] https://cointelegraph.com/news/ico-market-2018-vs-2017-trends-capitalization-localization-industries-success-rate

[15] Ring Signatures
https://www.getmonero.org/resources/moneropedia/ringsignatures.html

[16] cjsgo.com

[17] https://bitcoin.org/en/getting-started

[18] View more ATM statistics at coinatmradar.com

[19] Consumer Financial Protection Bureau
https://files.consumerfinance.gov/f/201408_cfpb_consumer-advisory_virtual-currencies.pdf

[20] https://en.m.wikipedia.org/wiki/African-American_businesses

[21] https://smallbiztrends.com/2018/08/african-american-small-business-statistics-2018.html

[22] https://moneymaven.io/blackwealthchannel/community-building/asians-keep-a-dollar-in-their-community-120-times-longer-than-african-americans-2ZvNTGNxpkClloXlXK_wMQ/

[23] Bitcoin volatility (BVI) has dropped from 15.6% to 2.4% since 2011.
https://www.buybitcoinworldwide.com/volatility-index/

[24]
https://en.wikipedia.org/wiki/Household_income_in_the_United_States#Racial_and_ethnic_groups

[25] Market where prices are rising, and buying is encouraged

[26] https://guapcoin.com/newsite/

[27] Open Bazaar https://openbazaar.org/

[28] Bit Happy http://bithappy.co.uk/

[29] https://www.pewresearch.org/fact-tank/2014/04/24/more-hispanics-blacks-enrolling-in-college-but-lag-in-bachelors-degrees/

[30] https://apps.urban.org/features/wealth-inequality-charts/

[31] Bitwage https://www.bitwage.com/

[32] https://www.theblockcrypto.com/2019/06/24/getting-divorced-splitting-up-crypto-assets-could-prove-a-headache-lawyers-warn/

[33] https://www.computerworld.com/article/3315696/blockchain-developer-salaries-now-command-as-much-as-175k.html

[34] https://moguldom.com/183278/morgan-state-partners-with-crypto-company-ripple-to-boost-blockchain-research/

[35] Users are paid based on their stake in the coin

[36] Report: Harvard, Stanford, MIT Endowments All Invest in Crypto Funds. https://cointelegraph.com/news/report-harvard-stanford-mit-endowments-all-invest-in-crypto-funds

[37] The Real Size of the Bailout

https://www.motherjones.com/politics/2009/12/real-size-bailout-treasury-fed/

[38] https://www.huduser.gov/Publications/pdf/unequal_full.pdf

[39] https://medium.com/@social_8123/these-wall-street-executives-are-leaving-for-big-time-blockchain-jobs-9a9d31c018ac

[40] Clovyr https://clovyr.io/

[41] Americans Paid $34 Billion in Overdraft Fees Last Year. Here's how to stop the charges.

https://www.forbes.com/sites/learnvest/2018/04/05/americans-paid-34-billion-in-overdraft-fees-last-year-heres-how-to-stop-the-charges/#7b577e703ce9

[42] https://www.wonderopolis.org/wonder/how-much-money-can-a-bank-hold

[43] https://www.watchtheyard.com/life/black-owned-banks/

[44] https://cointelegraph.com/news/silvergate-bank-onboarded-59-new-crypto-customers-in-q4-2018

[45] Exploding Cryptocurrency Use in Remittances From US: 15.8% Now Using Cryptocurrency

https://www.ccn.com/exploding-cryptocurrency-use-in-remittances-from-us-15-8-now-using-cryptocurrency

[46] Jamaican Stock Exchange to Pilot Bitcoin and Ether Trading

https://www.coindesk.com/jamaica-stock-exchange-to-pilot-bitcoin-and-ether-trading

[47] Akon Wants To Use Blockchain and His Cryptocurrency Akoin to Fuel a New Ecosystem in Africa https://www.newsweek.com/2019/03/08/akon-akoin-blockchain-cryptocurrency-new-ecosystem-africa-1339550.html

[48] https://www.newsweek.com/2019/03/08/akon-akoin-blockchain-cryptocurrency-new-ecosystem-africa-1339550.html

[49] South Korean Political Party To Use Blockchain For Member Processes https://democracychronicles.org/blockchain-for-member-processes/

[50] Meet The US Politicians Embracing Bitcoin

 https://www.coindesk.com/meet-the-us-political-candidates-who-are-embracing-bitcoin

[51] What do the Major Streaming Services Pay Per Stream

https://www.forbes.com/sites/hughmcintyre/2017/07/27/what-do-the-major-streaming-services-pay-per-stream/#1f58425b448c

[52] 50 Cent: "I Forgot" Taking 700 Bitcoins for 2014 Album; Stake now worth Millions

https://www.npr.org/sections/thetwo-way/2018/01/24/580259163/50-cent-i-forgot-taking-700-bitcoins-for-2014-album-stake-is-now-worth-millions

[53]] "Sats" is short for "Satoshis" the smallest denomination of Bitcoin

[54] https://www.coindesk.com/national-football-league-union-partners-with-blockchain-startup

[55] https://www.nba.com/kings/news/kings-first-sports-team-mine-cryptocurrency-establish-multi-year-scholarship-fund

[56 https://www.nba.com/kings/news/sacramento-kings-become-first-professional sports-team-accept-virtual-currency-bitcoin

[57] The Resurgence of Black Farmers

https://civileats.com/2016/07/15/the-resurgence-of-black-farmers/

[58] https://www.forbes.com/sites/brittanychambers/2019/04/15/one-founder-left-the-vc-world-raised-more-than-1m-in-crowdfunding-to-build-her-communitys-wealth/#56a8989821d3

[59] https://kevintpayne.com/top-vc-firms/

[60] www.blackchainonline.com

ACKNOWLEDGMENTS

First, I want to thank my mother, Belinda. Thank you for all of your ideas and encouragement. This book would not be possible without you!

I want to thank Sinclair Skinner, Max Keiser, Trace Meyer, Adam Bach, Andreas Antonopolous and the collective Bitcoin community for educating me about this amazing technology.

I want to acknowledge Dr. Claude Anderson, Nipsey Hussle, Percy "Master P" Miller, Ice Cube, Thomas Sowell, Malcolm X and Kwame Ture for helping shape my view of Black America.

ABOUT THE AUTHOR

Isaiah Jackson is the founder of multiple blockchain startups and a Bitcoin consultant that bridges the gap between cryptocurrency and consumers. He is currently the co-host of "The Gentlemen of Crypto" news show, a Certified Bitcoin Professional and Bitcoin evangelist since 2013.

Made in the USA
Middletown, DE
28 March 2021

36419578R00106